FROM AN EGG

Ray James

Rourke
Publishing LLC
Vero Beach, Florida 32964

www.rourkepublishing.com

PHOTO CREDITS: All photos © Lynn M. Stone except title page and #10 © Marty Snyderman

Title page: A horn shark hatches from its egg case.

Editor: Robert Stengard-Olliges

Cover design by Nicola Stratford.

Library of Congress Cataloging-in-Publication Data

James, Ray.
  From an egg / Ray James.
    p. cm. — (Let's look at animals)
  Includes index.
  ISBN 1-60044-172-6 (Hardcover)
  ISBN 1-59515-531-7 (Softcover)
  1. Eggs—Juvenile literature. I. Title. II. Series: James, Ray. Let's
look at animals.
  SF490.3.S764 2007
  591.4'68—dc22

                        2006012864

Printed in the USA

CG/CG

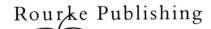

Rourke Publishing

www.rourkepublishing.com – sales@rourkepublishing.com
Post Office Box 3328, Vero Beach, FL 32964

Table of Contents

Eggs

Baby animals grow from eggs! Birds are not the only animals to make eggs. Nearly all kinds of female animals make eggs.

Animal eggs are very important.

Some animals **lay** their eggs, other animals do not lay eggs.

A sea turtle lays her eggs in a sandy hole.

Mammals

Furry animals, like people, are **mammals**. The babies of most mammals grow inside their mothers.

Almost all mammals are born directly from their moms. They begin life from a **fertile** egg, yes. But most mammals do not grow inside an **egg shell**.

9

Who Lays Eggs?

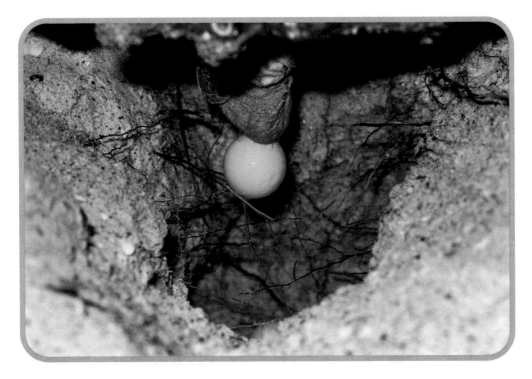

Many kinds of animals do lay eggs. That means the animal pushes the eggs out of its body.

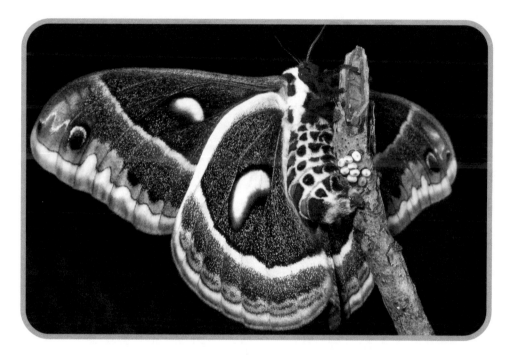

Insects lay eggs. Many kinds of spiders lay eggs.
Snails and oysters lay eggs. Many kinds of fish
lay eggs.

Different Eggs

Each animal's eggs are different. Eggs may be big or small, white or colored. Shells may be hard, like a bird's egg. They may be soft, like a turtle's egg.

Eggs even have different shapes. Some are very round, like little peas. Some are rounder at one end than the other end.

A chick breaks through the hard eggshell with its beak.

Some chicken eggs are brown and some are white. All chicken eggs have the famous "egg shape."

Many Eggs

An animal may lay one or two eggs or several thousand. An oyster can lay 100 million eggs in one year!

A male jawfish protects hundreds of eggs in his mouth!

Why do some animals lay so many eggs? Because other animals eat their eggs! Laying many eggs means at least some will survive.

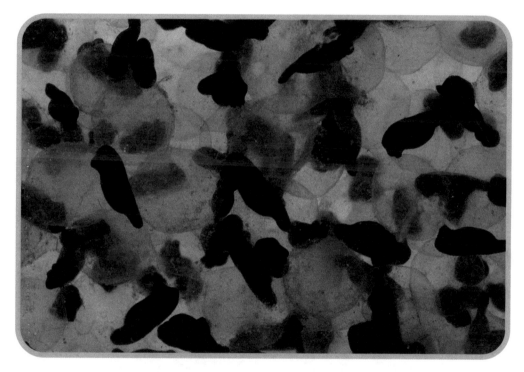

Frogs lay hundreds of eggs. Tiny frogs called tadpoles hatch from them.

Inside an Egg

What is inside an egg? Fertile eggs hold a growing baby animal. They also hold food for the growing baby.

The egg food helps the baby grow. Some animals grow faster than others do. Finally, the food is almost gone. The baby **hatches**!

Some new babies can live by themselves. Adults must care for others. Baby turtles are on their own.

Glossary

egg shell (EG shel) — the outer cover that some eggs have

fertile (FUR tuhl) — prepared to grow new life

hatch (HACH) — to break free from an egg shell or any egg covering

lay (LAY) — to push an egg out of the body, often into a nest

mammal (MAM uhl) — any of the animals that make mother's milk and grow hair

Index

FURTHER READING

Gill, Shelly. *The Egg*. Charlesbridge Publishing, 2001.

Morgan, Sally. *From Egg to Duck*. Chrysalis Books, 2002.

Taurel, Alison. *Animals and Their Eggs*. Gareth Stevens, 2000.

WEBSITES TO VISIT

http://www.saczoo.com/3_kids/17_eggs/_egg_layers.html
http://www.calicocookie.com/eggsunit.htm

ABOUT THE AUTHOR

Ray James writes children's fiction and nonfiction. A former teacher, Ray understands what kids like to read. Ray lives in Gary, Indiana with his wife and three cats.